DEFYING EX

DEFYING
EXTINCTION

AMY BARONE
POEMS

Broadstone

Library of Congress Control Number 2022936903

ISBN 978-1-956782-11-0

Text & cover design by Larry W. Moore
Cover photograph by the author

Broadstone Books
An Imprint of
Broadstone Media LLC
418 Ann Street
Frankfort, KY 40601-1929
BroadstoneBooks.com

For Harold Bollaci and Achille "Kelly" and Mary Barone

CONTENTS

IV Love & Family

V Anima Protection

I

SACRED PLACES

SURVIVORS

Cahows re-emerged on Bermuda's Nonsuch Island
after a 300-year absence. They thrive amid
native flora, wildlife, and limited access to man.

Tangier Island in the middle of Chesapeake Bay
supplies the world with soft-shell crab.
Where water defines life, where home and country matter.

The piping plover, hailed one day each summer
for its resurgence in the Rockaways, New York,
lives protected in camouflaged nests on the beach.

Shadowboxing Arctic hares, clinging jellyfish, bonebeds
and badlands on Fossil Freeway in South Dakota.

Me—I'm the woman with medicine in her voice
a forest bather mating like a corpse plant, melting into time,
floating toward a twelfth life like a trumpeter swan.

Sanctum

Some places need no name.
Like the local bird sanctuary,

a two-acre park
bequeathed to Haverford

by an eccentric neighbor.
Where an emerald carpet

studded with hundreds of trees
and blueberry bushes

is rolled out for heart-weary visitors
like an ethereal shrine.

STRAWBERRY MOON

The vibrant low moon shadowed a day flooded with sunshine.
How many in this city, teeming with tourists and bustling locals,
more attuned to their iPhones than a Native American celebration,
knew it marked the start of the hay harvest?

In Manhattan, Kansas, by the light of a moon tinged orange-yellow,
farmers rose at 4 a.m. to prep for a day of cutting and baling feed.
Just as the Algonquins, on reserves in the Ottawa River Valley,
once gathered strawberry roots and leaves in the brief season to brew potions.

Nature-devoted poets fired up their computers to pen odes to the Solstice.
Saturn, in the glow of the "Rose Moon," nearly brushed elbows with Earth.
A slight hush fell over New York City as spring handed summer the torch.

ENTRANCED

Swathed in bright white clothing,
descendants of the Americas' first slaves
fervently pray to their *orishas*
until they fall into a trance.

A woman approaches the moored boat
as I anxiously watch from the tour bus.
Candomblé comes alive in the Yoruba tongue.
Many Catholics embrace it.

In Bahia, Brazil's land of happiness,
Salvadorans mix religion
with black magic and revelry,
where the Atlantic is wilder, the stars more intense.

FULL MOON OVER CAIRNS

Kangaroo dreams were shaking my sleep,
so I took the Muse Down Under.
My verse needed a shot of nature and color,
my head craved a new sense of place.

Thoughts of tropical heat in early spring
and music-filled nights made four flights bearable.
Despite ugly reports, the Great Barrier Reef breathes.
Residents in brilliant hues of green, orange and blue
circled our boat.

Lone sea turtles surfed underwater.
Coral, dancing and still, spoke to us.
Far from shore, a whale waved hello.
Near dusk, a flock of fruit bats flew low
as we strolled from McGinty's Pub.

A tropical mist coated the indigo night.
Dark clouds floated below a black tattooed moon.
Immersed in shrill silence.
Cairns, like a calyx, growing thorns to keep us still.

Island Exiles

The Tremiti Islands enchanted on our one visit.
Pinewoods, glistening grotto waters, the coves on San Domino,
and St. Mary's Church with its rare Byzantine cross.

We arrived by hydrofoil from Termoli, a city on the Adriatic,
where a street honors my second cousin Cleofino Ruffini
and the Swedish castle in old town houses his tomb.

He was a World War II hero gone too soon.
Longing to return one day, I set out to honor
the magical place and memory,
but altered mindscapes intervened.

I discovered that in 1334 pirates ransacked the five islands.
Centuries later, Mussolini rounded up Italy's gay men,
created internment camps, kept the citizens confined
on the once-glorious Tremiti Islands whose vistas had changed.

Happy People

They christened each day with breakfast at the piano—
a group of blissful people singing and laughing.

I was on vacation in Santo Domingo with my sister,
cradling my heart at twenty-two after a failed affair.

Harboring little appetite, I was smoking Marlboro Reds,
drinking El Presidentes and losing money at blackjack.

But the singing intrigued me, propped up low spirits.
Oh, they're the Venezuelans said the hotel manager
as the spry clan returned to their perch at Happy Hour.

Hard to conjure up those echoes of cheer when a nation,
a wildlife haven, land of tasty *arepas* and the grand Angel Falls,

today has people fleeing or waiting in 12-hour lines for food,
bringing their own supplies to hospitals, starved for hope and joy.

HEAVENLY PARK

At day's end, when the sun's myriad campfires recede,
light a torch with the fire Prometheus seized
and join me at a Dark Sky Park.

Earth's hot. A new plague landed. Nightfall is safer.
Maybe we'll find remnants of a shiny meteorite
to hang at home.

I'll fix a moonrise picnic on a beach of stardust
with a view of Andromeda and the Milky Way,
while we can, before the stars explode.

Cosmic beauty may portend the end—the Big Crunch
or Big Rip or Quantum Bubble—dark energy isn't loyal.
It may catch us unawares, between bites of barbecued tofu

or between breaths, as we gaze at the North Star.

Swimming on La Luna

A yellow ribbon of angst floats above.
During the lockdown, some spent days
baking bread, while a friend nearly starved
to death—driven to the ER by fear and seclusion.

A magnet for benign and wicked misfits,
I pull a mask over distress, pluck thorns
from my sides, and spend fitful nights
asleep with people still in my system.

Now that water's been spotted there,
I think I'll head to the moon for a swim,
embrace lunar life off the grid, get revived
on a smooth intergalactic ride, as I wave goodbye
to bugling elk, dazzles of zebras, and dozing cuttlefish.

Mars Bound

Though I recoil from lines, I'm standing in one,
intent on moving to Mars.

Surmounting fear of flying to make
an eight-month trek on the Virgin mothership.

Throw 35 million miles between us,
pass over blue states, red states, too much talk,

the fuss that festers when walls go up.
Awaiting red mountains and lakes, new seasons.

Resolved to erect a life unfettered
by wires, rules, love, and reason.

II

THE WILD

TREE TALK

Baltic temples
in forests
lured people
to release sorrows
and setbacks
to the trees,
protectors, shade, our friends.

Twilight Flight

After the sun drops,
a cobalt dusk takes root.
Leaves in ochre, saffron
and jade float toward night.

Vestiges from the maidenhair tree,
symbol of love and longevity.
Venerated as sacred and strong.
Distant cousins survived Hiroshima.

Traces of emerald horizon and brown shadow
give way to blue tattooed sky.
Fan-shaped bodies of foliage,
their delicate veins like seams of a quilt,

find safety in numbers, reach for partners
as they sway and prance.
Emboldened by a twilight dance,
they grow larger beneath chameleon heavens,

bringing breezes and calm,
celebrating day's end,
beckoning us to dream,
in color and touch find peace.

BEARLY

Abruzzo's Brown Bears,
calm creatures who roam
the Apennine Mountains and woodlands,

summer in meadows up high
and sleep on branch mattresses by day,
are at risk of extinction.

Fifty Marsican bears, activists for ecotourism,
remain—to search for beloved Buckthorn berries,
embark on twilight *passeggiate*,

near the land of my ancestors
in a grand national park on a tourist-ridden
peninsula that's in hibernation.

BRONX BUTTERFLY

A tiny shock of orange sashays above traffic.
I hope she's leading the way.
East Fordham Road and an Indian summer day

coated in brilliant sunshine. Bookish destination:
a library off Arthur Avenue to honor my heritage.
Past café-lined streets that sing in Italian,

where cannoli are filled to order—custard or crème.
Sadness and sickness circle secluded friends.
Hoping poetry can restore us all,

and this flecked butterfly,
my guide on the journey,
will help lighten the weight.

CICADA SHOALS

They last swarmed in 2004,
one of the sunniest years of my life.
The wine flowed.
For everything that I treasured, I still held hope.

A young jazz drummer came courting.
Cheered on by my sister and late mother,
I took the stage for my first poetry solo.
That night we all glowed.

I no longer sleep with ease
and now the buzzing land shrimp are back.
In the billions—dubbed Brood X.

I hear their eerie whirring all day.
On sidewalks, I navigate their countless remains.
One lay on my terrace overnight.
When I went to remove it, the cicada came alive.

As their adults pass on,
the babes will burrow underground
and I dream of joining them in a 17-year sleep.

The Canary

A yellow cardinal was spotted
yesterday in Alabaster, Alabama.

The news flew across Facebook and Twitter.
The rare-hued bird garnered fast fame.

Yet skin tone renders some creatures hidden.
Others invisible. Whether they want to be seen

and heard or not.

A Love Supreme

He trudged upstairs to pray for days.
Descended in rapture, armed with a four-part suite.
John Coltrane's saxophone blares "Acknowledgement."

He chants to McCoy Tyner's cues.
"Resolution" swings and screeches:
agape lives and matters.

Elvin Jones on tympani amplifies the faith.
In an Afro-Cuban beat, "Pursuance" embraces grace.
'Trane gives fellow travelers a bonus track:

poetry of gratitude played out in the notes of "Psalm."
Sanctified sounds from the '65 vinyl poured from windows
on spring nights in "The Haight."

Plethora of gifts from a man and his horn.
Turning water into wine. Parched listeners sated.

QUEEN OF TONE

Abigail Ybarra didn't live nine lives.
She stopped at one.

Her job spanned over 50 years at Fender Guitars
where small nimble hands of a Latina teen made waves.

A pickup winder, she advanced from work in soldering and lit
a path for other young women who found joy in a unique job.

Striving for brilliance, "her" electric guitars mesmerized
legions of fans and radicalized the sound of rock music.

She drew demand from Jimi Hendrix, Joan Jett, Eric Clapton,
who relied on her handcrafted pickups for their edgy sound.

A legacy with measure: they say she wound guitar wire
that would have circled the world 16 times.

IN THE POCKET

Pockets make life lighter.
They once wielded power, were taboo for dames.
But their true value springs from the groove.

Music empowers listeners to reach heights,
like the time Stanley Clarke and Lenny White jammed
at the Blue Note one breezy fall night, wrapped in swing.

Or that '87 Andy Summers show when I was surrounded
by "it" girls on and off stage at Philly's Chestnut Cabaret.
Rosie Vela strutted her Texas stuff in red Botticelli curls
and sass, singing "Tonto" and "Magic Smile."

The ballads oozed rhythm and blues. A short-haired
honey blonde in the crowd entertained a harem of hot men.
I snaffled these scenes for years. Out of pocket no more.

KANGAROO LOVE

You sustain
like kangaroo grass,
a life-giving grain.

The first bread
whose survival grows
stronger with fire,
especially in spring.

Tall and blonde,
always a bit parched.
Leaving me too breathless.

Rest Stop

At a river's edge, a baby elephant suckles his mother.
A small herd meets, then trudges through water, trunk-to-tail.

On a golden field at an animal rest stop in Kruger National Park,
water buffalo, zebras and gazelles

are caught unawares doing what nature dictates.
An eagle overlooks his fiefdom from a bare tree perch.

Alligators languish on their turf.
A hippo's yawn could fill a photo frame.

Grinning penguins pose, safe from zoos and loud tourists.
Birds in exotic blue and orange feathers strut.

A rainbow crisscrosses Victoria Falls.

TREE GHOST

Riveted to trees, snow and sky, he rocks
a maxi cape of gold and brown feathers,
flaunts a fresh manicure.

A creature without a strong star,
but I thought that mattered little.
His silent amber eyes compensate.

Speaking through off-balance ears,
the hoot of a wise man with killer instinct
ventures out at dusk.

He shuns sleep. Spurns allegiance.
Prefers anonymity when hunting.
Mistaken for a ghost, this beast alarms

visitors to cemeteries where a magical
wind always blows and prey thrives.
The face of many I left behind.

ULTIMATE SPA DAY

Today they will be coddled and massaged.
On hearing the news, friends and family rushed
to spoil them with pedicures, hair care and words of comfort.

Now sporting lustrous manes, the horses
at Masterpiece Equestrian Center who munched
on tainted feed earlier in the week, will leave with love.

No remedy exists to treat their dying muscles,
so young owners flock to the stable to administer
one last blast of touch and whisper "farewell."

GETTING IN TUNE

Surviving takes practice.
It took decades to know

you were better off without them.
Though Italians are supposed to love family.

Tunes tingle memory.
Less can be best.

Break rules.
Tear down the walls of exile.

Expel the darkness
like bees do every spring.

Build the cue. Banish the muse.
Write for a few.

Date music, not musicians.

III

HEIRLOOMS

SACRED ROCK

Pouty-mouthed figures with ribbony arms in majestic and languid poses
fill the rooms of Pace Gallery. Many recall the sharply-chiseled face
of Abraham Lincoln. Some wink, others hide eyes. I meet *The Aristocrat*,

Hades' Head, and *Cave Girl*. Hallowed in precious white rock from Carrara,
where anarchy boomed in the 1800s and ex-convicts and fugitives worked
      the mines.
Dangerous work still. But marble thrives. Retracing Michelangelo's steps,

an Irish artist travels to Pietrasanta at the foot of Tuscany's Apuan Alps.
He builds trust with families whose artisan studios eschew machines.
Kevin Francis Gray sculpts from a prized resource that glitters in raw form.
Fashions his version of David.

MEDEA'S CAMEO

I wonder if Medea wore a coral cameo
when she embarked on the journey
with Jason seeking passion and gold.

A brooch revealing Athena on a raised relief,
an ancient campaign button of hope,
an amulet for an enchantress who divined.

Under a watery sky, did she dance
to wind songs on the hunt for treasure?
Did she regret her treatment of the King?

Love is love—it nurtures and heals.
But pride can trample hearts.
And when revenge turns gruesome,

a magical charm can't stop a blazing rage
that ignited more than her soul.

ANALOG HEART

I trust time from a turquoise travel alarm
powered by an AA battery.
I chill wine in an old GE freezer that doesn't make ice.

In a rush and a mood to splurge, I flag a yellow cab,
disheartened that a "gig economy" promising driverless cars
drove a bankrupt livery driver to die at his own hands.

I don't watch movies from a Smart TV that may be watching me.
The music I stream pours from NPR radio, giving airplay
to a mix of young, hungry and brilliant artists.

Sometimes I draft stories on paper, not a blinding screen.
Soft on the eyes and gentle on my low-tech mind.

Missing Spice

I sprinkle chaat masala on most dishes now.

Craving travel and adventure, I shun bland herbs
and embark on excursions that begin and end in the kitchen.

When I miss lulling train rides, I indulge in chamomile tea
as I shave ginger onto stir fries and eggs.

On holidays, in a nod to Mediterranean roots, I ration scoops
of white truffle oil for fresh pasta, relishing the pungent tang.

I cool my tongue with anise seeds, pour a bitter *digestivo* over ice
whenever the jolt from turmeric and serrano assaults.

As the urge to journey heats up, I play Motown sounds and move
to upbeat tunes as I edit the list of places I long to savor.

THE HEAD NUT

Aromas of French roast and Ceylon cinnamon intoxicate.
Barrels of nuts and spices fill the store, where I unearth
hard-to-find ingredients. Cash or checks preferred.

I'm lured by a pile of Easter candy whose sugary thin wafer,
when I was a kid, reminded me of Communion hosts.
Strips of red licorice transport me to my father's den
where he kept a stash of sweets in a drawer.

As traditional retailers fold, replaced by virtual stores,
I make treks to The Head Nut for kitchen staples.
Service with a smile and welcoming chitchat.

Dried papaya in summer. Italian chestnuts in fall.
Bargain weekly specials. A coffee bar serves as rest stop.
Civilization as I like it—slowly vanishing in American towns.

HOTEL SEVILLE

Its Beaux-Arts crown will continue to impress passersby,
since it's no longer destined to make way for a new luxury dorm.
The landmarked hotel lives on by Madison Square North.

Haunting green bay windows remain,
take me back to somewhere sweet.
They once welcomed single ladies traveling solo
when the practice was thought a bit shocking.

Sand-hued limestone lion heads and foliage
survived a century of noise and wear.
Its red brick façade stands tall in a city
of glass skyscrapers lacking heart.

A Tiffany skylight adorns modern décor.
Years ago, once inside, I looked out
while dancing to *forro* sounds at a Brazil Day bash.

Now when I walk by, especially at dusk,
I linger to gaze at grandness, listen to its music.

PIANO ECHOES

We stream music and view YouTube.
Outgrew our stereos and CDs.
They had tune-smiths at their pianos
playing rollicking sounds.

Music filled the alleys of New York's West 28th Street.
Father of the Blues J. C. Handy and Scott Joplin wrote
catchy songs there in the early 1900s.

Ragtime and jazz poured from saloons and halls.
Where "In the Good Old Summertime"
and "Give My Regards to Broadway" were born.

A universal language took root.
Walls to show biz success fell.
America's sheet music trade thrived.

When in a good mood, my late father used to sing around the house.
He'd belt out, "Hello! Ma Baby," an old song to a young girl
who loved rock music, who knew little of Tin Pan Alley's past splendor.

HANDKERCHIEF

Mementoes of a gentler time—crisp cotton handkerchiefs
edged in lace, some stamped with embroidered flowers—
perfectly pressed, piled in drawers at my late mother's home.

As a child learning to iron, I'd choose the square plaid hankies
my father carried to work and the white ones he used in church.
Handkerchiefs once held cachet.

A wave with one across the room signaled attraction.
At the Roman games, they heralded the official start.
They were bequeathed to loved ones in ancient Egypt.

Othello's first gift to Desdemona was a hankie.
As early as 77 B.C., Catullus weaved them into his poems.
In Gone with the Wind, Rhett handed Scarlett one in a dramatic scene.

I found a paisley handkerchief in my mother's handbag
on the day of her stroke. I left it there, cherished it,
never to be handled again—a symbol of etiquette,
her ladylike ways, a vanishing age.

The Bell Museum

She spoke through a bell
after the stroke stole her voice.

A decorative brass bell that once sat
on a bookshelf with no aim became her mate.

She preferred the company of friends
but few made time for my mother

now that she couldn't treat them to meals,
chat on the phone in her sweet tone; the laughter.

So I was moved to discover the Malmark Bell Museum,
housing bells that graced churches, school music rooms, town squares.

In 16th century England, handbells were used to send messages,
as my mother communicated in her last years.
Etched with feathers and teardrops, the bell now sits on my desk.

CHARM BRACELET

A tiny ruby chip marks the date of her wedding
on a 14K gold calendar for July '57.

Three facial silhouettes etched with her girls' names and birthdates.

A Christmas tree decorated with red, pink and blue-jeweled balls.

San Francisco's Golden Gate Bridge; her monogram on the back.
She was never one to waste space.

A big round smoky topaz in a stunning gold setting, fit for a queen.

A scene of Athens' Parthenon—a place she'd never visited
and I dreamed of seeing.

The number of her first homeroom, H.R. S30, at Chester High School.

A tiny gold music box that plays "I'll See You in my Dreams."

IV

LOVE & FAMILY

CLEMATIS

Reluctant like a clematis,
I shy from conflict
with a fragile friend.

Purple with passion,
how do I tell a mentor
I can't bear his demands?

I relish sunshine on my face,
but drift to calming shade.

Once I knew how to climb,
kept my reach high on the vine.

Now I mingle with wild artists,
crush the impulse to wilt over rows.

TALONE'S YARD

The slight pear tree held
my five-year-old curious-girl frame.

Fall fell year-long.
Ladybugs tempted and purified.

Startled by a praying mantis, I dropped to my knees.
A doorway in the hedge led me home.

Years later, I finally learned to inhale.
Half-smoked cigarettes dotted spots under the pines,

where I also left my innocence. Baited by bases.
Kissed by the sun. Sustained by drugstore candy and dreams.

BEAUTY PARLOR

At Peg and Sue's beauty salon,
we sat listening to the radio for the numbers.
My mother under the hair dryer,
her salt and pepper curls in big pink rollers.

Me on the floor paging through fashion
and women's magazines dreaming of glamor
and straight blonde hair.

Here housewives gathered for their weekly wash-and-set
amid the scent of permanent wave solution.
Manicures were a treat for special occasions.

All worried for Jude Plum who was eligible
for the draft—the Vietnam War raged on.
So many now gone.

Today, Jude runs a chic hair salon
in a more upscale section of town
catering to cancer patients and survivors.

GRIPPED BY THE EDGE OF NIGHT

I learned the facts of life at the foot
of my mother's ironing board
each afternoon as we followed *The Edge of Night*.

Sex was more mysterious in the 1960s,
but I understood its essence. The show's dapper
Adam Drake awakened my crush penchant.

Transfixed by handsome actors that filled
the black and white screen, watching soap operas
made me want to grow up fast and get married.

So I practiced during kindergarten,
until my mother received a call from a teacher saying
that I was spending too much time in the playhouse.

The soaps taught me how to cope with stress:
head to the crystal decanter and pour yourself a stiff one.
If you need to take more of the edge off, light up a cigarette.

The Edge of Night had a 30-year run.
I can still picture Monticello's indigo cityscape on the screen
and hear the dramatic theme song with its strong piano.

NEST

Day after day
the robust robin
dives into the potted tree

of sheer leaves and flimsy branches.
Chooses the same time I seek inspiration
from the changing scene outside a nest,

furnished with my late mother's treasures,
home to spirits who lure me to stay and bear witness.

PAINT JOB

I'm foregoing a vacation to paint my late mother's home.
Maybe fresh coats of bright white will brush away the betrayal,
trauma, loss that inhabited the rooms in her last years.

I'll go with blue in the bedroom, sky blue
to bring some of the heavens back inside a place
that once shined with my mother's spirit and smile.

Buttery yellow, like the Easter coat I wore as a child,
for the empty dining room. It once held a mahogany table
that served a young family of five, but the bulky furniture
blocked the terrace light beaming in sunny mornings.

Al said he'd even touch up the laundry and closets
where her classy clothes once hung, dissolving stains of rage,
residues of illness that created family seisms.
I'm trusting a palette of pastels for closure and renewal.

SECRET FLIGHT

The word "travel" is linked to "travail" meaning "work" in French;
a "tripalium" is a three-staked instrument of torture used in Ancient Rome.

The dark family secret sailed
on a long slow journey.

It started back when travel lured, invigorated,
kept me absorbed in a place.

A diminished world, spinning faster and faster,
made a dent. But the secret stayed dormant.

A tale of infidelity, indiscretion, lust
that I should have kept buried, but instead confided

when trust and longing triumphed.
It came to rest on my mother's ears as she lay dying.

I could see the shock in her eyes and silence.
The secret revealed in a whisper by my sister,

who once caroused with me in Sedona, Acapulco, Rome,
before the stress of delays, long lines, missed connections.

Message

She hovered outside my bedroom window
one steamy morning in July.
I barely recognized her with wings spinning,
nose prodding.

As I pondered whether to begin the day.
But she vanished and my mind drifted further.
In August she returned, singing from her bright
blue throat as if an urgency awaited.

My mother relished nature's dance from this window.
She saved news clippings of successful writers for my visits.
A petite sugar-lover who fiercely guarded her abode. Adored music.
Revisited to relay a message I continue to decode.

Resting in Peace?

Flags flutter.
Breezes hug.

School kids screech
from the asphalt playground
across the street.

I lay aside dark thoughts
as I enter this quiet spot.

Parents nearby,
fragrant grass,

fields of flowers brought
to loved ones
not forgotten, but honored

in a personal shrine,
as they rest and await
company.

HALF MOON

Come down from the cross.
Unglue your hands.
Bandage your neck.
Forgiveness is overrated.
Live well.
Don't pay the ultimate price for
their trespasses.

The Trees Remain

I found the Black Angus that used to graze
on Bryn Mawr Avenue. They're hiding
by Saw Mill Road since housing took their land,
clustered under tall trees that keep our secrets.

Pennsylvania skies speak to me
when thoughts turn away from you.
A slice of light across the horizon
sandwiched between dark clouds
draws me back to an elusive touch.

Late afternoon flashes golden light
on bare treetops and evergreens,
a snapshot of your smile.

Shuttered shops and waning community
on our Main Street find me alone
with shadows and wind.

A fiery sun still sets where we used to indulge
in nothing by the duck pond.
Sheltered by trees that stayed, that take longer
than stars and some loves to die.

V

ANIMA PROTECTION

Defying Extinction

The ribbon will be massive.
Proof that no lady died in vain.

I add a piece of sky-blue fabric from bedding
my late mother sent me as a housewarming gift.

Others brought cherished family linens, baby clothes,
and delicate doilies. A writer weaved in a purple silk blouse

to create a memorial that will hang along the Brown Building
in Lower Manhattan, where 146 garment workers

at the Triangle Shirtwaist Factory perished in a fire
on March 25, 1911—one of the nation's worst work disasters.

We honor mothers, wives, sisters, daughters and friends, plus 17 men,
who worked with their hands, mostly immigrants in a new land.

Escape blocked by locked exits and stairwells. Their sacrifice propelled
activism, dignity for workers, remembering.

GHOST DANCE

Abandon the battle—join me at the Ghost Dance.
Embrace silence—quiet movers change the world.
Fall into a trance.

Peace calls for a circle, joined hands.
Listen to others' demands—stifled speech
breeds tyranny. Grab your shield and feathers.

From Nevada to Idaho to Wyoming and the Dakotas.
Some dancers survived Wounded Knee in 1890.
Wovoka carried on the mission—true identity.

Redemption warrants risks. A savior awaits.
The commandments hold sway. An afterglow
fortifies and heightens hope for tomorrows.

villa in Tivoli.
uidly.
ow?

es, story-telling, the Eternal City.
lovers and fickle friends.
ar; *write of the heart's traitors, not politicians.*

ver 2000 years,
and fall of Rome,
e writing lessons.

PETALS

They're watching me.
I relax; this is where
I'm meant to be.

Teaching a class,
reading poetry,
explaining why

and how I create.
Relating to students
in night school

middle school
from foreign lands
foreign streets

foreign beliefs.
But in the moment
we're community.

Their intent faces
reveal trust;
we unearth chemistry.

My words the beacon
of this peace.

ENSNARED

She returned to the place where she first
experienced longing and surrender.

Where past loves had been tangible as mercury,
elusive as ghosts.

By day, butterflies clung to spikes of blue veronica,
crimson azaleas filled in bright green bushes.

At night, dazed and glowing with a moon tan,
she caught the sole pulsing star,

then tossed her shillelagh, vowed to engineer life's voles
on her own terms.

Wizard-ess

It's all in the timing.
You have to keep the game in play as long as possible.
Gauge your investments—coin gets eaten fast.

Most times what you see is what you get.
Unless you're hiding under a glass dome like I used to do.
I'd let them tilt me too low, bump me too hard.

Then I learned to trap them—became an expert at
manipulating steel balls, holding them in place
using my brain, not my hips.

So they would nudge harder and get locked out.
I scored my way into multiple replays.
Balls piled up in the drain.

I never limited myself to themes, as I like most music.
Now I'm relaxing, resting my sharpened flippers.
Anticipating my next visit to the arcade.

PIECES OF A DREAM

Shards of faces slip beneath me,
over me, through me.

Glimmering visions in black and white or three colors.
Ones I no longer love appear.

My mother, in the apricot dress
she wore to my sister's wedding, liquefies.

Flashes of computer screens call me to task.
I'm playing a digital game I don't understand.

I walk down familiar streets
in cities I no longer know.

Taboo Dream

I dismount the white horse,
abashed and drenched in shame.

A seesaw in the distance evokes days
of innocent slides.

I swing thoughts to those times,
helpless to flick a kickstand down

on an unscheduled ride.

FORGETTING

Friends and lovers should be stamped
with an expiration date to forewarn us
when the end approaches.

I need to brace myself better for betrayal,
a nasty outburst, the Monster rearing his head.
So to sharpen the art of forgetting,

I enter a small room that overlooks
a tangle of trees and orange azaleas.
Warmed by an *espresso macchiato*,

I struggle to remember the magic
that touched this gypsy soul.
And stay locked away until I erase

the how, the why forever.
Then I vow to take faith in the now
and head to the River Lethe for a swim.

MINDSCAPES

Bewildered by blazing bridges
where friends played, then betrayed.

Is it him? Is it her? Or did I set the flame?
No need for alarm. The dead impart the best advice.

I turn to carillon sounds to heal.
Search for seasons that didn't appear.

I appeal to the skies for need-less allies.
Reach for rare breezes before Mother Nature liquefies.

Calculating how many more poems,
when I should transform into bamboo.

Blood Orange Days

It's the beginning of spring.
Damp days and spirits echo winter.
Working remotely, I wait for the phone to ring.

Familiar noises have dimmed.
Neighbors on walks timidly greet or cross the street.
Trees are shrouded in white wisps.

The wind stopped whining.
A weathervane that hasn't moved in days
shifts south.

Reports of illness and death pepper my Facebook feed.
I grieve with Giovanna, an Italian friend in Brooklyn,
who buried her father and uncle in Bergamo from afar.

Poets vittoria Ripetto and Bob Barci have passed on.
Little Italy butcher, Moe Albanese, shy of 96 years, is gone.
People crave communion.

In other cycles, yellow daffodils stand tall.
The perfume of violet hyacinths evokes
a calmer time in a bigger world
when travel meant weekends at the Jersey shore.

Pink blossoms on Japanese maples
and weeping willows color the town.
The sun's shadow shelters leafless trees.
A sole ambulance siren slices the peace.

Dark Shadows

The menace coils toward virus-laden air.
It shrieks in wild riots and cities aflame.

Relentless storms uproot trees and darken streets.
An earthquake struck North Carolina after 100 years of calm.

Thick noxious smog stifles fresh breezes.
I look for refuge in eerie-colored skies that weep.

The pest silently divides on Facebook and Twitter.
A game of dominoes ends badly.

I walk 'round treeless circles where the sky is wide,
hoping, hunting, but not a cornflower to be found.

Lunar Love

They say her hidden side is dark,
but it's simply far. Locked in tidal swells,
she shows us the same face every night.

An asteroid passed close to earth
on the first day of spring
during the last supermoon.

She loomed high above the softened ground
where earthworms rose up to feed famished birds.
Selenophiles, we flaunt our love of the heavens.

No cure exists for our fixation.
A gold globe or yellow slice of sky.
The stars and moon stay true night after night.

Redemption arrives on cloud-filled days when she hides.
Or afternoons when her straying spirit burns bright.

WONDER

Galloping at full speed with no fear—
The haunting song I still want to hear—

The smile of a stranger who rescued me in a cable car—
A warm vibe that I've been here before—

That fiery red sunset that whisked me from a dismal road—
A shooting star before the sky explodes—

Healed.
Heartened.
Mystery.
Memory.
Wanting to stay.

BARDO

They're up there—in transition,
sandwiched between old and new lives.
Floating, attachment dissolving, thoughts turning pure.

They'll become who they're meant to be,
as long as they have the grit to conclude
unfinished business. Journey on.

The next time I chat up clouds of horses and unicorns,
I'll be more respectful of friends and family.
Speaking to stars is never in vain.

Dolce Far Niente

I miss what once was
and a little of what followed.

My houseguest, Grief, returned to Rome.

Plague-filled air has cleared—
fear compelled me to do little,
an Italian art I'm mastering as I reboot.

I breathe out like the trees—join them
in search of safety. I shop for food like a star-nosed mole.

A magical sky casts spells.
On the striped horizon, treetops glow.
In the beyond, scientists give a nod to black holes.

Christmas lights in Bridgeport twinkle in reveries.
We were happy then despite the ceiling cracks
and moldering beams.

Most nights, quarantine dreams intoxicate me,
so many people I hadn't seen in years.
I honed the power to make ghosts appear.

Now it's time—to own them—own it.
Recharge your smartphone—
freedom's on the line.

ACKNOWLEDGMENTS

The author gratefully acknowledges the editors of the following publications where these poems appeared or are forthcoming:

brevitas Anthology — "Bronx Butterfly," "Cicada Shoals," "Entranced," "Kangaroo Love," "Mindscapes," "Nest," "Resting in Peace?" "Taboo Dream," "Twilight Flight," "Wonder"

Brackish Daughters-The Politics of Shelter Anthology — "Sanctum"

Chelsea News — "Hotel Seville"

First Literary Review-East — "Half Moon," "Tree Talk"

great weather for MEDIA — "Lessons"
Suitcase of Chrysanthemums Anthology

Home Planet News Online — "Analog Heart," "Clematis," "Happy People," "Heavenly Park," "Lunar Love," "Mindscapes," "Paint Job," "Petals"

Jerry Jazz Musician — "A Love Supreme," "Piano Echoes"

Live Mag! — "Wizard-ess"

Local Knowledge — "Secret Flight," "Tree Ghost"

Long Island Sounds Anthology — "Full Moon Over Cairns"

Long Islander Newspaper–Walt's Corner — "Queen of Tone"

Lowestoft Chronicle — "Missing Spice"

Maintenant — "Dark Shadows"

Muddy River Poetry Review — "Defying Extinction," "Island Exiles"

Narrative Northeast — "Survivors"

New Verse News   "Swimming on La Luna"

North of Oxford   "Ensnared," "Medea's Cameo"

Orbis #194   "Heavenly Park," "Lunar Love"

Otoliths   "Getting in Tune," "Pieces of a Dream"

Ovunque Siamo   "Blood Orange Days"

Paterson Literary Review   "Charm Bracelet," "The Bell Museum"

Philadelphia Poets Literary Journal   "Bearly," "Bronx Butterfly," "Gripped by the Edge of Night," "Island Exiles," "Mars Bound"

Poetry Ink Anthology   "Full Moon Over Cairns," "The Head Nut," "The Trees Remain"

RememberTheTriangleFire.org   "Defying Extinction"

Red Wheelbarrow   "Handkerchief," "Piano Echoes"

Sensitive Skin Magazine   "Survivors"

Silver-Tongued Devil Anthology   "Message"

Standpoint Magazine (UK)   "A Love Supreme," "Bardo," "Full Moon Over Cairns," "Ghost Dance," "Rest Stop," "Sacred Rock," "Strawberry Moon," "The Canary," "Twilight Flight"

Tamarind   "Mindscapes," "Pieces of a Dream"

White Rabbit Tribute Magazine
To John Ashbery and Colette Inez   "Sacred Rock"

Wild Violet   "Talone's Yard"

Thank you to Larry Moore, Sheila Bucy Potter, and Stephanie Potter of Broadstone Books for the publishing opportunity and for your contributions to the world of poetry. A huge thank you to my editor, Patrice Adcroft, for your expertise, friendship, and unwavering support. I am immensely grateful to writer friends and boosters—Davidson Garrett, Ron Kolm, Maria Fama, Patricia Carragon, Karen Neuberg, Cindy Hochman, Susana H. Case, and Joey Nicoletti. Many thanks to members of the brevitas online poetry community, which provides a canvas for many of my poems.

About the Author

Amy Barone is the author of *We Became Summer*, published by New York Quarterly Books (2018). She wrote *Kamikaze Dance*, from Finishing Line Press, which recognized her as a finalist in the 2014 Annual New Women's Voices Chapbook Competition. Foothills Publishing released her first chapbook, *Views from the Driveway*, in 2008. Her poetry has appeared in *Local Knowledge*, *New Verse News*, *Paterson Literary Review*, *Sensitive Skin*, and *Standpoint* (UK), among other magazines and anthologies.

She spent five years as Italian correspondent in Milan for *Women's Wear Daily* and *Advertising Age*. Barone has worked as a communications director at non-profit, government, and private organizations. She holds a Bachelor of Science degree in Business Administration from Villanova University and a Master degree from the Thunderbird School of Global Management.

Barone is a member of the Poetry Society of America and belongs to the brevitas online poetry community that celebrates the short poem. She performs at spoken word events at venues in New York City, Northern New Jersey and Philadelphia. A native of Bryn Mawr, Pennsylvania, she lives in New York City.